Homebuilt Clocks

by

Gary F Hartman

Published by
Gary F. Hartman
Lebanon, OR

Homebuilt Clocks

Copyright © 2011

By Gary F. Hartman

All rights reserved. No part of this book may be reproduced or transmitted in any form, or by any means (except for the inclusion of brief quotations in reviews) without the prior written permission of the author.

ISBN 978-0-9815399-3-5
Library of Congress
Control Number 2011903337

Printed in U.S.A. By Lightning Source Inc.

Foreword

After building nine or ten clocks in a style similar to those described in this book, I decided such projects might be of interest to others and therefore would be a topic for a new book. This book will provide a guide to construction and allow a craftsman or builder/ woodworker to fabricate a very nice Grandmother style clock, as well as adapt to other styles.

The work involves fairly straightforward woodworking skills, and the use of tools like the Table Saw, Router, Jigsaw or Sabre Saw, wood chisels, and other basic hand tools.

Safety is a prime issue with any such work; the use of safety glasses, a dust mask and ear protectors is essential.

Once the basic clock is assembled, finishing is next; actually I find it takes as much effort as building the clock... but the book shows a technique that provides a very nice result similar to fine furniture finishes.

Often various woods are used, with some, like Oak and Ash having distinct grain patterns. But others have faint or other patterns, requiring some Art and painting tricks to accomplish a nice grain match in the finished clock. In all cases, picking wood with unique knots and swamp rot will add distinctive beauty to the work.

For example, fancy manufactured moldings required are sometimes only available in Hemlock or similar woods, with virtually a non-existent grain. I use India Ink and a brush and fine Crow Quill pen to simulate an approximate grain pattern to match to the Oak and Ash; in Art sometimes you only hint at an effect you desire and the eye completes the illusion. This is the purpose here, a few wipes, or inked grain here and there and the effect is quite amazing.

My hope is a builder can simulate the effect and achieve a good result- and I have confidence they will.
So, I wish a reader well and hope he achieves a beautifully finished clock.

>Gary F. Hartman
>Lebanon, OR
>www.jgenasplace.com

Other Books by the Author:

"Kids' Book of Adventure Projects" 2008

"Homebuilt Firearms" 2010

Table of Contents

Chapter 1   Overview, Construction, Safety..............1

         2   Parts, Inner Box ……........................5

         3   Basic Moldings for the Clocks.............14

         4   The Bottom Molding........................22

         5   Building the Top Molding...................27

        6   The Door Assembly...........................35

        7   Finishing the Inside............................51

        8   The Clock Finish................................57

        9   Final Assembly of the Clock................67

       10   Mantel Style Clock.................................69

Chapter 1

Basic Construction,
Tools and Safety

The basic construction of the clocks incorporates a wooden inner box, with various moldings and add-on decorative pieces to make each clock unique and attractive. Use of several tools is required, especially for the custom upper portion above the dial. Depending on the style, a mantel or wall clock; the lower moldings will be totally different, but usually is made from a purchased prefabricated fancy wall baseboard type molding .

If it is a wall mount clock, the base piece will taper attractively inward below the bottom of the main box assembly; if a mantel clock, the bottom molding will extend outward to support the clock above as a free standing unit.

Figure 1 gives a rough idea of initial construction for a Grandmother Style Wall Clock.. Essentially the base is reversed for a mantel versus a wall style clock and the mantel clock should be shorter, probably with a smaller overall size and dial diameter, etc.

Look at Figure 1. The inner box is very basic; there is no need for fancy furniture joints here unless you are a true woodworking craftsman and simply enjoy doing that sort of construction. The joints should be square but do not need to be rabbeted or keyed, etc.; in fact with the pieces being thin, you are better off to use inner corner bracing for a little extra strength.

I usually used 1/4" Oak veneer plywood for the sides, and 3/8" Oak veneer or even common Luan plywood for the top, bottom and rear portions. The reason for using the 3/8" is lighter weight, but also for adequate thickness to allow for small finish nails to be used in construction. 1/2" plywood would also work but at the cost of a heavier clock.

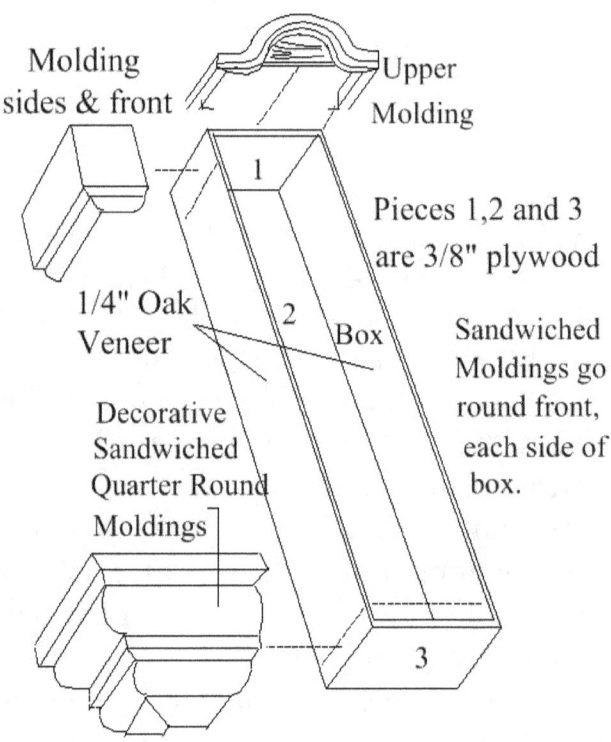

Fig.1. Basic Clock Body

Figure 1 shows some of the moldings, giving an idea of the effect of the decorative pieces. Later drawings will discuss them in more detail. Sometimes making two moldings with the router and sandwiching them together forms a very nice effect, and that process really adds to the look of the clocks discussed in this book. Not shown is the tapered bottom moldings, but those will be discussed later. Always try to pick a workpiece with a knot or rot spot for uniqueness.

For the other major moldings and decorative parts of the clock outside the box, I use Ash or Oak. I prefer Ash as it has an Oak like grain pattern and finishes as nicely as Oak; it matches fairly close to the Oak veneer plywood, etc. It also works better than Oak, with less splinters peeling off when routing. Oak is also acidic; nails and screws will corrode in Oak. Often you can smell the acid odor as you cut it.

Of course the wood you use is your preference (to perhaps match to some existing furniture.)

Always use a damp paper towel or damp cloth to wipe excess glue from a glue joint. Stain will not absorb into a surface if glue is present.

Tools Required, Safety

Tools required for these clock projects are those an experienced woodcrafter would normally have: a Table Saw, perhaps a tilting Radial or Cutoff Saw, and a Router with bits, sanders, clamps, some wood chisels, square and measuring tape, paint brushes, wood glue, hammer, screws, nails, etc.

The builder taking on these projects should be experienced with the Router and Table Saw. **These are extremely dangerous tools, and require experience and care in operation.** Their use is necessary for these clock projects, and it can be pointed out over and over that care and skill and SAFETY are critical. BE SAFE!!

Points on Safety

A few notes on safety, critical for a person doing cutting, sanding, routing; all the activities required for these sort of projects:

- **<u>ALWAYS</u> <u>unplug the power cord when changing Router bits or any saw blades</u>!! <u>ALWAYS</u>!!**

- ALWAYS use safety glasses or a face shield.

- ALWAYS use ear protectors and a dust mask when using power tools.

- When doing finishing, spraying, varnishing, etc. use safety glasses, good ventilation and a mask for spray mist!

- **During any cutting or routing be EXTREMELY careful, a moment of distraction could spell disaster. A saw blade or router bit can inflict instantaneous damage or amputation. Clamp the workpiece securely!**

- **Do not wear long sleeves if there is a chance of the clothing snagging in the tool..**

- Regularly clean up your work area; you don't want to trip over scraps or have something cause an injury to you or others.

- Simply think through each process ahead of time and try to avoid a mistake. **Be SAFE!**

Chapter 2

Ordering Parts,
Getting Started,
The Inner Box Assembly

The construction described in this book is for Grandmother style wall clocks with a few comments in the last chapter on mantel clocks.

As discussed in Chapter 1, this is a very simple box. The sides are 1/4" Oak veneer plywood. The back and top and bottom are 3/8" Luan Mahogany or Oak veneer plywood; both are commonly available from any lumber supplier. Often, you can get half sheets, which are plenty long enough for these style clocks.

Otherwise, if you use full sheets, be careful as you run panels through the table saw, get someone to help you!

Never worry too much as to the clock height as long as the side panels are 30" to 34" high; that will usually be adequate unless you are using one of the Tempus Fugit or Moon phase type dials with the additional half circle at the top. In general, for a round dial clock 30" to 34" is entirely adequate.

Another factor is important in firming up on clock size- you must pick your dial diameter. The scale of your clock is based upon the dial size. This basically sets the clock width as the dial must be visible within the door frame, which is typically on the order of 1 1/2" width on each side, with glass inside this frame.

I have found several suppliers of clock parts, some of them have the preferable dial size for a Grandmother Wall Clock, others may have a smaller size more suitable for a mantle clock..

<u>Typical Part</u>
<u>Suppliers</u>

Norkro.com, Portland, OR
for motors, dials, hands, weights, etc.
1-503-292-2884

Klockit.com, Lake Geneva, WI
for motors, hands, small dials, brass weights
1-800-556-2548

Clockparts.com, Culver City, CA
for larger dials, motors, hands, weights
1-888-827-2387

For a typical Grandmother Clock, the perfect sized dial is metal, brass finished, about 7 7/8" diameter described as "Fancy Clock Dials", either in Arabic or Roman Numeral. Each character is on an individual white background circle, which really sets them off nicely. See Figure 2. Pick hands in a 3 1/2" or close size.

The motors are an Electronic Westminster Chime with Pendulum movement. They run for at least a year on one "C" battery. When you purchase such a motor, you also pick a free set of hands in your style choice and the pendulum and hanger to go with it. A Brass washer, rubber washer and nut are also supplied with the motor.

As you pick the motor, you must pick the dial shaft length to allow going through the dial back plate, (in these clocks that would be ¼" Oak veneer plywood...) and protrude about 1/2" above, this equates to about a 3/4" shaft length. Keep this in mind.

Photo courtesy
clockparts.com

Fig. 2. Fancy Clock Dials

The pendulum diameter for a Grandmother Clock should be the 3 1/2" size. (For a smaller Mantel lock, a 2 1/2" should be about right...)

The pendulum hanger is usually about 16" long with one inch break-off nicks to adjust to shorter lengths.

Brass Shell weights come in about 5 inch lengths and 9 inch sizes. The large ones would be suitable perhaps for a larger clock, like a Tempus Fugit type dial with the Moon portion above the dial, for others, the 5 inch style is fine. They come with brass finish chains. The shells are for attractive appearance only, they are non functional.

So that leaves us with a typical set of parts:

- Motor, Westminster Chime, Pendulum Type
- Dial, metal, Fancy Arabic or Roman, 7 7/8" Diam.
- Hands, approx 3 1/2" set,
- 3 1/2" Pendulum and Brass hanger,
- Brass Shell weight set, 5 inch length. (2 per set..)
- Get some small Brass hooks at a hardware.
- Ornamental Brass Hinges, Stanley type 80-3460, Liberty 76XC type or similar, three needed.
- Brass Hook and Staple, Stanley 803640

The Basic Box

See Figure 3. With a dial of about 8" diameter, the full width of the clock should be about 11 inches. A 7 to 7 ½ inch depth is perfect.

So you will cut two side panels of 1/4" plywood, with grain

running lengthways... approximately 7" wide x 30" to 32" long. Use a fine tooth plywood blade in your table saw, so as not to damage the edge of the thin plywood.

Next cut the back and top and bottom pieces, of 3/8" plywood, either Luan or Oak veneer. It is not critical, the top and bottom will later be covered with a specifically cut Oak veneer piece to hide the Luan. Take care that all corners are square and true.

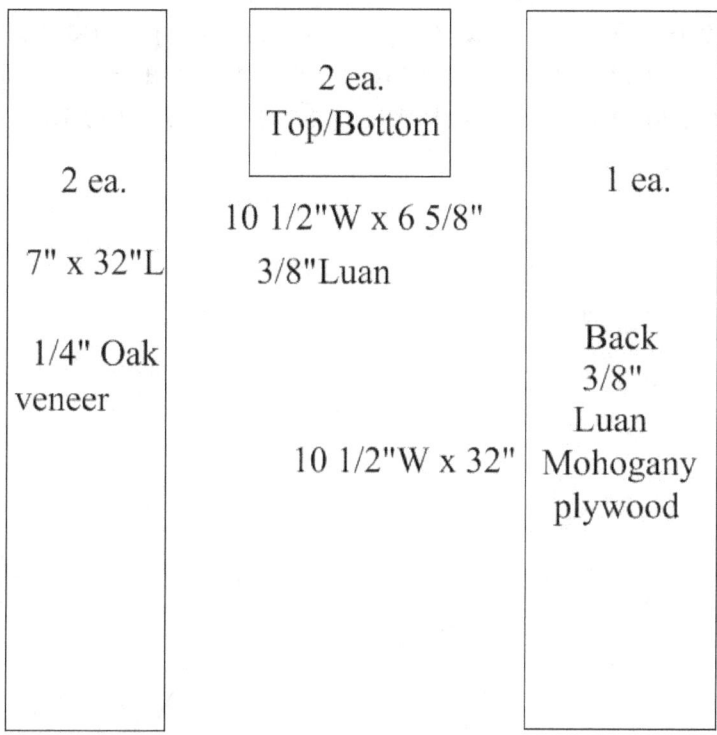

Fig. 3. Basic Box Parts

Assemble the 3/8" pieces first using carpenters' glue and 7/8" 18 ga. finish nails. Use two wood clamps to form a bottom support base to hold the top and bottom pieces upright as you lay the back on them and glue and nail the back to the ends. With the top and bottom pieces on the shop floor, apply glue one at a time; align the back carefully and then nail through the back piece into the top and bottom pieces.

Use a Nail Set Punch to set the nails. Wipe excess glue from the joint inside and out with a dampened paper towel..

Next remove the clamps and tip the assembly onto its side. Apply glue and carefully align again and place one side panel on, Oak veneer to the outside. Nail with the 7/8" 18 ga. finish nails. Set the nails. Wipe off excess glue with a damp paper towel.

When doing the last side, place a few newspapers beneath the first veneer side to protect it. Once finished, be sure to wipe any joints free of excess glue.

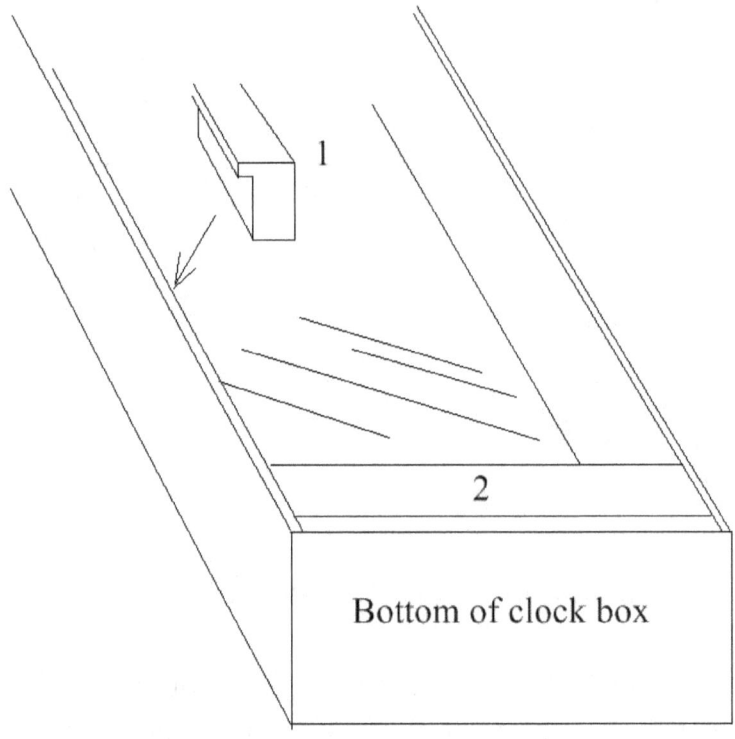

Fig. 4. Details of Trim

There are two remaining items for the box, a support trim on the edge of each 1/4" side, and a crosspiece at the bottom. See Figure 4.

The side support trim is cut from a soft wood, like clear pine. Pick a nice clean board, (no knots...) at least 3/4" thick and 3" to 4" wide or so (4" wide specified boards are nominally 3 1/2" wide..) First you will end cut it to fit perfectly for length inside the clock box. Or cut slightly long, and trim to fit later...

Next, run both edges of the board flat through the table saw with the blade height adjusted to form an inset that is just the thickness of your side veneer, 1/4", leaving about an eighth inch portion at the top untouched. Then readjust the blade height and tip the board on each individual edge to run through to remove the inset, leaving the small lip to fit over the side veneer of the box.

You now should have the board with each long edge cut to form a notch looking like 1 in Figure 4. Next use the table saw to rip down each side edge to give about a 5/8" sideways thickness for each molding.

Trim the length, and check that the pieces fit nicely on each side and cover the exposed edge of the Oak veneer. Then glue and clamp, wipe off excess glue with a moist paper towel. When clamping, use a scrap board or two against the sides to apply even, continuous pressure along the length of the trim. These trim pieces will strengthen the edge and provide backing for later adding the door hinges.

Next, cut a piece of solid wood, (2 in Figure 4.) 3/4" thick and about 1" width to a length to just fit snugly between the interior at what will be the bottom of the clock.. Apply glue on three sides, set into place, clamping and wiping off excess glue.

Allow the glue to dry.

I like to use dowels for strength. You can drill matching 1/8" to 1/4" holes into the veneer sides and perhaps about 3/4" into the bottom cross piece to allow an end dowel joint at each end of the bottom piece. Use a scrap of masking tape on the drill bit as a depth gauge. Once drilled, measure into the hole with a sharp awl and then use this depth to cut two dowel pieces to glue into the holes. Once again wipe off excess glue. These dowels apply a significant strength to each end joint.

Cut some 6" long approx 3/4" x 1" scrap blocks to fit into each corner of the clock box, as corner braces, and glue them into the corners of the box. You can use rubber padded bar clamps kiddie-corner to apply gentle pressure during gluing. Or cut some thin slats to prop between the box sides to apply a gentle pressure as the glue dries. If they are cut slightly long, they can bow a bit to apply a small pressure.

Once dry, remove clamps, and turn the clock body on its face. At the end you will have as the top, (opposite the crosspiece you dowelled in....) Measure down in the exact center about 10 inches, and mark and drill a 1" blade bit into the back surface until the tip is through the plywood and the blade bit is just into the surface. Then turn the clock box face up and drill from the front to complete the hole.

Turn the clock body face down again. Use the router with a clamped board as an edge guide along with a 1/8" veining bit to rout a centered groove straight and true towards the top of the clock box, about 1" long from the 1" hole . Adjust the depth about 1/8" deeper on each cut until you have the groove cut through the 3/8" back..

Widen the slot slightly on each side by moving the router edge guide a tad. This forms a centered slot for aligning the clock onto a wall support screw when mounting the clock. Test with a 3" deck screw or similar to be sure the screw shaft will slide into this slot, but the head will hold the clock.

This completes the basic clock box/body. See Figure 5.

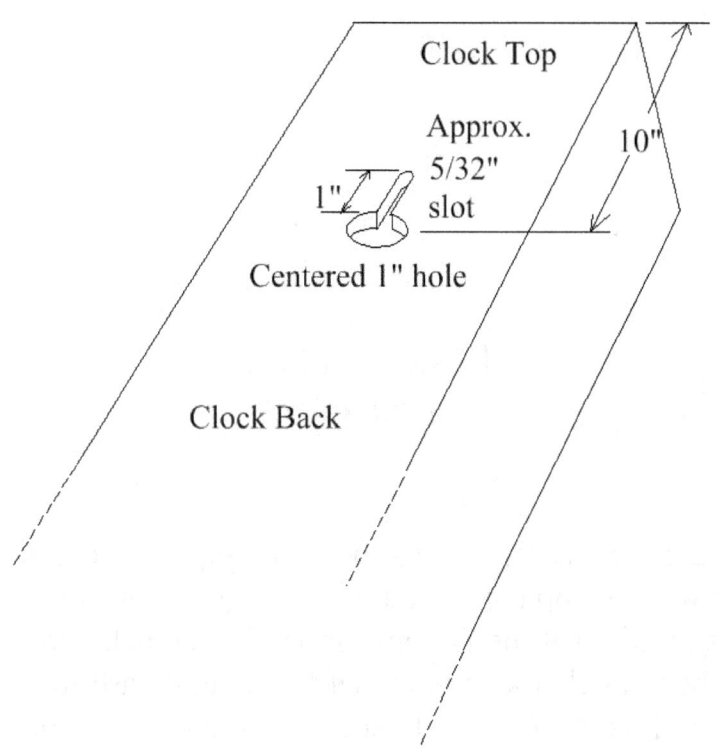

Fig. 5. Hanger Slot

Chapter 3

Basic Moldings for the Clock

    There are three areas of the clock that require decorative moldings. As we develop them, you will recognize that a different approach is required at the bottom for a mantel clock versus a wall clock. The mantel clock requires a substantial base for stability. The base will taper *outward* to supply this support. But the wall clock bottom molding is tapered *inward* for a decorative effect.

    Moldings at the bottom of the wall style clock are of two types, one is a purchased, fancy baseboard or corner style, available usually in Hemlock; the other is made of two routed, then sandwiched quarter round moldings.

    One quarter round molding can be done on one edge of a 4" wide length of Ash, (typically this wood comes in a 7/8" thickness..) the other on the other edge. Now, one edge will have a fairly *wide* lip as in Figure 6, but the other routed portion will end up being fashioned to result in a *narrow* lip edge. This requires routing one edge with the board flat, and one edge with the board upright; also lengthwise saw cuts are required to narrow the thickness of the one edge and achieve a molding design.

    This process achieves a very decorative molding once the pieces are sandwiched together and glued. The final effect is shown in the combined molding in Figure 6. This is an easy process for a straight type molding, as we have at the bottom of the wall clock, and it is very attractive on the finished clock..

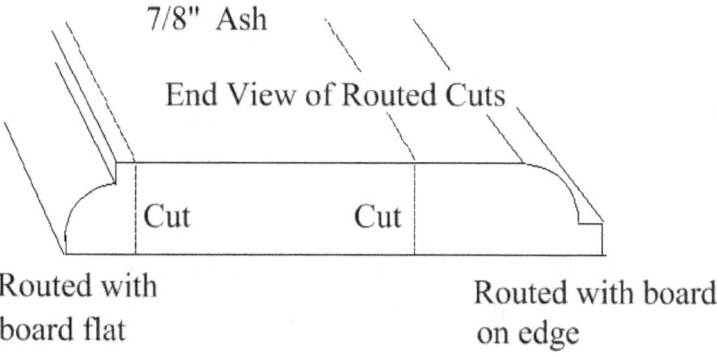

Use 3/8" Rounding Over Bit

Once routed and cut as shown, rotate the left portion and glue and clamp to the right portion.

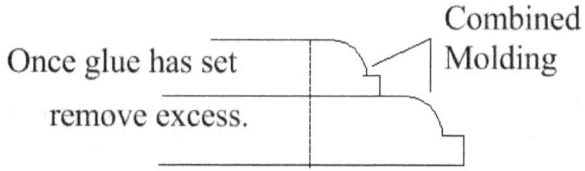

Fig. 6. Upper Bottom Side/Front Molding

Figure 6 shows the appearance of the fabricated molding; it is actually inverted and corners mitered to form the upper bottom molding.

Next look at Figure 7. This is a variation of Figure 6, another option giving a slightly different, but also usable molding.

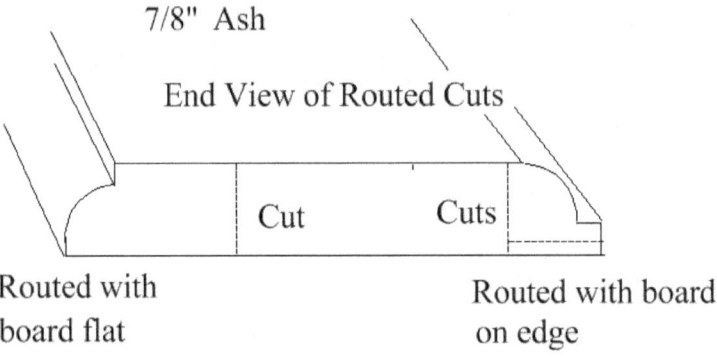

Use 3/8" Rounding Over Bit

Once routed and cut as shown, rotate the left portion and glue and clamp to the right portion.

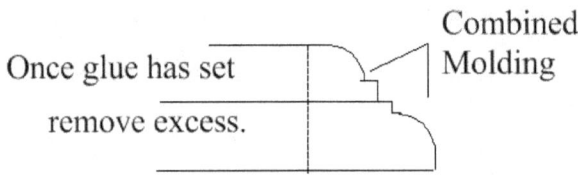

Fig. 7. Another Molding Variation

As you can see, there are numerous possibilities here, each attractive in appearance and all possible using the same basic bit with the router ...but rotating and fastening them into a single thicker, wider molding. As you study them you will see how you can easily do a variation with simply one bit and the router; now add to this the possibilities of other bits, a Cove bit for example.

Further, you also have the option of variation with the upper clock molding, where you can devise various curvatures, which you will route to form the decorative upper clock shape. Thus you achieve uniquely different clocks by simply allowing your imagination to flow with different ideas.

When routing these pieces, keep in mind safety. You need to be confident and careful with this tool! Maintain control.

- Make the pieces longer than you will need to allow clamping securely as you work. The piece must be long enough for each side of the clock plus the front, with a large allowance for mitered corners.

- Be sure the edge of your workpiece is smooth, it will be the surface the bit guides on during the last cut.

- Grip your router very securely.

- Make light cuts on each pass, gradually working inward towards the final cutting position, where the lower guide portion of the bit rides right against the edge of the workpiece.

By adding possibilities with a cove molding you have additional results.. See Figure 8 for a photo of several actual molding shapes. The lower right molding is a fancy baseboard molding style with an added block to give a taper. This one is excellent for the tapered bottom molding . To its left is a sandwiched combination as we have been discussing . Above are two Round Over bit samples. And at the top is another type fancy corner molding.

Make two routed moldings of your choice with a stepped portion as shown at each edge of a 3/4" to 7/8" thick piece of Ash or Oak,..about 4" wide.. make sure the entire piece is long enough to accommodate for the two mitered corners. (This will require a total length of about 35 to 36 inches...) Then cut and sandwich into your choice of molding. Glue and clamp, wiping off any excess glue with a damp paper towel.

Fig. 8. Molding Samples

When dry, slightly trim the inner portion "W" of the molding even and true by running it through the Table Saw. Measure the width "W" of the molding as it will mount on the clock. Multiply this by 1.5 and add this amount to the length of each side to give an allowance for including the miter corner. Then set up for a 45 degree miter corner cut, and cut this accurately at one end. Measure and cut the rear end straight across.

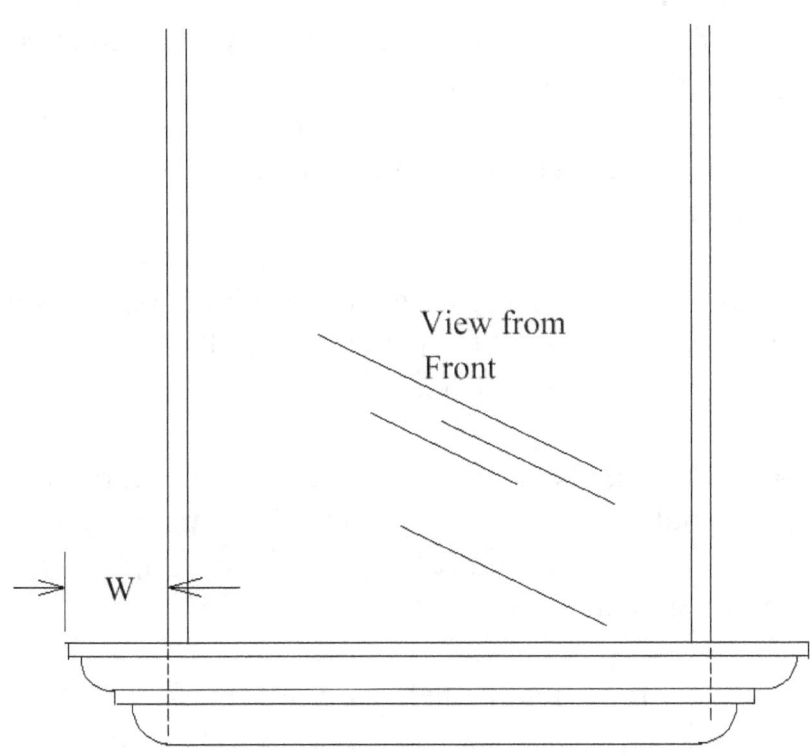

Fig. 9. Width of Molding

Do the second side piece in like manner, mitered corner, etc.
The remaining piece is the front, requiring two true mitered corners 45 degrees. Cut one end at the correct miter to allow

mating to one side molding. Clamp the matching side molding on temporarily and see if the mitered front slides accurately against it. Fine trim if not a perfect match. Then mark and cut off the rear of the side molding to match to the clock depth. Do not cut off front molding excess yet, cut the other end to the 45 degree miter to match the other side piece. It will be too long, but you need to check its miter match to the other side piece before cutting it to the perfect length.

Remove the first side piece and clamp the other side molding on to check its corner match... if it does, you are set, otherwise adjust your Table or Radial Arm Saw slightly and trim to get a match. Keep the saw at this setting.

Once this angle is correct, you are ready for gluing the first side and cutting the final front molding length. Two points to keep in mind:

- Allow a 1/4" overhang below the clock bottom.. this is to allow for positioning the bottom tapered molding inside the lip, which comes later.

- Apply glue and clamp the first side molding carefully in place, butt the front molding to it to be sure it is correctly positioned. Wipe off excess glue with a damp paper towel. Do not glue the front molding piece!

- With the front molding held carefully, mark the inside of the molding at the other front corner. Using your saw recut the miter close to this point, allow a hair extra, you can fit perfectly when you glue the second side piece in place.

Once the first side molding has dried, set the front molding against it and check with the other side molding as you fine trim the front molding length to make the joints perfect. Remove excess side molding overhang at the back after trimming and perfecting the front fit precisely at the corner.

When you are satisfied with the miter joint you may set up the second side molding, and glue into place, positioning it with the front also clamped to hold a precise fit. clamp, clean off excess glue. You may choose to go ahead and glue the front molding on also.

This will complete the first molding placement. Prior to moving to the next chapter, drill a 1/8" or 1/4" hole into the upper side moldings of each front corner to allow dowel reinforcement of the molding corner joints. Cut two dowels and glue into the dowel holes. If you wish, you may also drill and mount dowels at the rear of the molding into the clock body. Wipe excess glue off. Next is the tapered bottom molding.

Chapter 4

Building the Bottom
Molding

In the last chapter shown in Figure 8 were two fancy baseboard or corner moldings suitable for the tapered bottom molding on the wall clock.. The idea is to do the miter cutting for the two corners with the molding *tilted.* Thus it will be very decorative plus unique. Remember it was instructed to leave a 1/4" lip at the bottom of the side and front moldings... this essentially gives an outside guide, which holds the fancy tapered molding in position.

A special support block inside will provide strength to support each side of the moldings at an angle. Look at Figure 10 on the next page to see a view of where this is heading. You can see the molding just described in the last chapter above the bottom tapered portion.

The photo does not show a bottom plate yet, however a 1/4" Oak veneer will eventually cover the bottom. There will be braces inside, hidden to support the angled molding as well as the bottom Oak veneer. The wall clock is not meant to rest on the tapered bottom; it is for an attractive appearance, but the bottom will still be quite strong when complete. There is essentially a hidden hollow compartment beneath once the clock is finished, but you can cut a small slide fit cover or glue it closed, your pref-

Fig. 10. Bottom Clock Molding

erence. It works best to make the support braces that mount beneath and glue them to the back of a long strip of the fancy molding to set the 45 degree taper angle as they will eventually mount. Then the miter corners can be cut on the Table or Radial Arm Saw. That way when the moldings are finish assembled and fitted beneath, they will tilt to form the taper; the miters will fit nicely and the whole package will finalize the bottom of the clock..

See Figure 11, which shows a rear view of the braces, the interior supports. There are three, one for each side beveled molding and one for the front. The supports have a 45 degree angle cut as shown along their length . You can do this on a long strip of scrap wood running it through the Table Saw. *Make sure* your strip of molding and support piece will be enough for all three sides including miters.

Be extremely careful with any cutting, do not wear anything that can catch in the saw blade; keep the saw unplugged until ready to cut. Wear ear, eye and breathing protection.

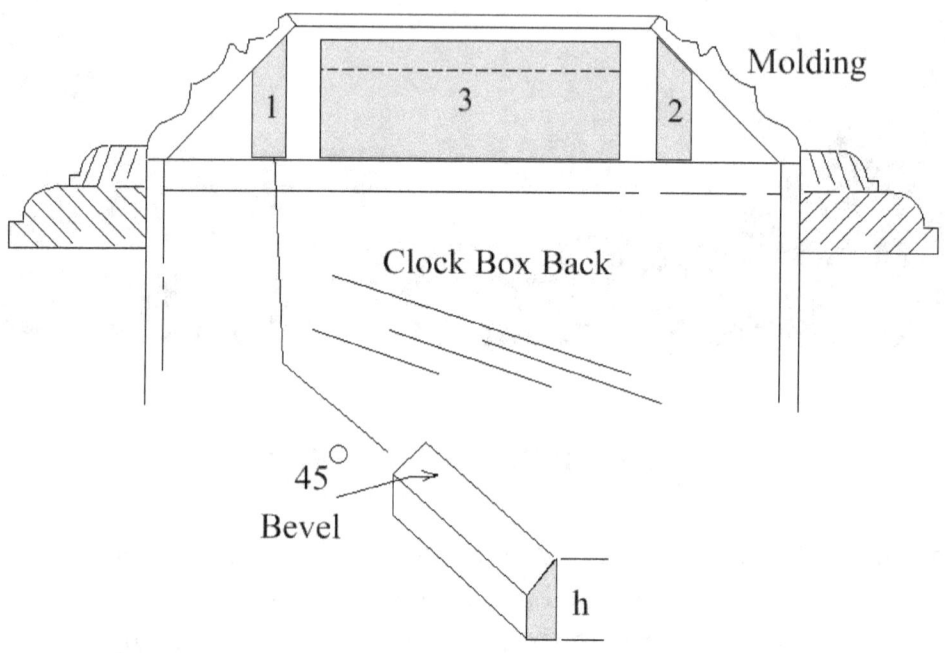

Fig. 11. Bracing for Bottom Molding

Cut the support height "h" to adjust for a pleasing 45 degree slope of the fancy molding when the support is near the edge of your molding as shown. Then glue it along the molding prior to cutting the mitered corners.

You will now have a long molding strip, with a tilt. By cutting the mitered corners afterwards, you will achieve a nice tapered bottom molding.

Be careful to cut the miters in the correct direction, check lengths and fit against the clock bottom as you cut each one. Once all three are cut to the correct fit and miters matched, you can glue them on. Stand the clock upright, bottom up and apply carpenters' glue. (Apply glue between the miters as well.) Place a bit of weight on a scrap board set across the moldings. Be sure to wipe off excess glue that could show on the outside finish.

Next, cut some braces from scrap to support a 1/4" Oak veneer across the bottom of the clock. Set the height to the correct amount to give good support inside at the left and right edge. These pieces should recess into the opening leaving a 1/4" space for a fill in piece on the back of the clock. The idea is to bevel the 1/4" oak veneer piece to fit smoothly into the bottom hole, sanding carefully to achieve a nice smooth fit around the edges. With the supports beneath on each side adding strength, this will allow gluing around the bevel edge as well as to the supports. Take care test fitting, and once satisfied, apply glue to the supports and edge, then with the clock upright, again apply a weighted board to the the bottom veneer.

Your final job should appear as in Figure 12 on the next page . You can add a fill in piece to the back to inset into the hole, either as a secret compartment, or glued it in solid.

Fig. 12. Finished Bottom Decorative Molding

Chapter 5

Building the
Top Moldings

The top molding for the clocks is an artistic design, pretty much at the hands of the builder. I suggest looking at several styles in various clock magazines, catalogs, ads, etc. to get some ideas. In general they are made up of curves, and multiple curves, the idea being to form some sort of attractive shape extending outward at the top from the clock body... a molding that protrudes to complement the bottom decorative moldings.

In my clocks, I have not tried to glue sandwich forms to build more depth, it is much more difficult with the curve type moldings. And the single moldings do look nice without getting into the more elaborate work.

Initially you will build a straight sub molding, which lies beneath the curved molding. This is nothing more than an approximately 3" wide piece (about 3/4" thick..) of straight Ash (preferably...) or Oak with one routed edge to face downward and run around the front and each side of the clock body. Use a long piece that can extend around the three sides, including the mitered corner.

Clamp and rout one edge with the rounding over bit. After routing, cut to form the three pieces with mitered corners to make up the three sides. Check and fit the miters, and once you are satisfied, cut the length flush at the rear and trim the front to a perfect fit. Glue and clamp, wiping off excess.

It is a good idea to dowel the moldings, just to insure strength because the moldings tends to be the lifting point when hoisting the clock onto the wall or while handling during the remainder of construction. Generally use a 1/4" dowel or two to join the front corner miter of the inner sub molding and at the rear on the inner sub molding into the clock box sides. Drill both these into the side moldings to keep the front clean of dowels. See Figure 13.

Fig. 13. Dowelling Top Sub Molding

Next is the curved molding. This moldings is to be done carefully and with sharp bits, using slight and successive cuts to avoid damaging a complex part. You can get into segmented, glued together or pieced moldings to make the grain mostly tangential to the cut, but I have found you can also do careful cutting and cut the shape out of a single board. Make the piece a few inches wider than the clock to allow for clamping while you route the piece later.

You must first develop your pattern in a size to extend a couple of inches beyond both edges of the clock width. You probably can do a half pattern using a coffee can lid or some large container to achieve some combination curved patterns, and then make a mirror image for the other half by tracing . Try to make the top to bottom thickness of the curve as even as possible.

I mostly draw a pattern freehand and eyeball it but probably a mirrored method is more accurate. Study the clocks shown in Figure 14 next page for some examples of different moldings.

Once you have a full size pattern, mark it onto your workpiece. Use Ash preferably, it is far less prone to splintering during routing. Initial cutting of the shape is done with a Jigsaw, *run below full speed with a fine narrow blade to allow for cutting a curved path..* Running at a lower speed allows following the curve more easily. Cut slowly and carefully. Keep the space between the matching curves equal as possible on your entire cut.

With the basic shape cut on both sides, use a Belt Sander and hand sanding to smooth the surface of the curves. Be especially careful not to accidentally flatten a nice arc. Practice a bit on a scrap to get the feel and choose the grit for this job. Both top and bottom edges must be smooth and as evenly spaced as possible, especially keep the bottom smooth, it will form the guide for your router cuts.

Rip cut a long straight Ash board of the same thickness and width as the end portion of your curved front. This will be for the side pieces, and leave spare length once again for mitered

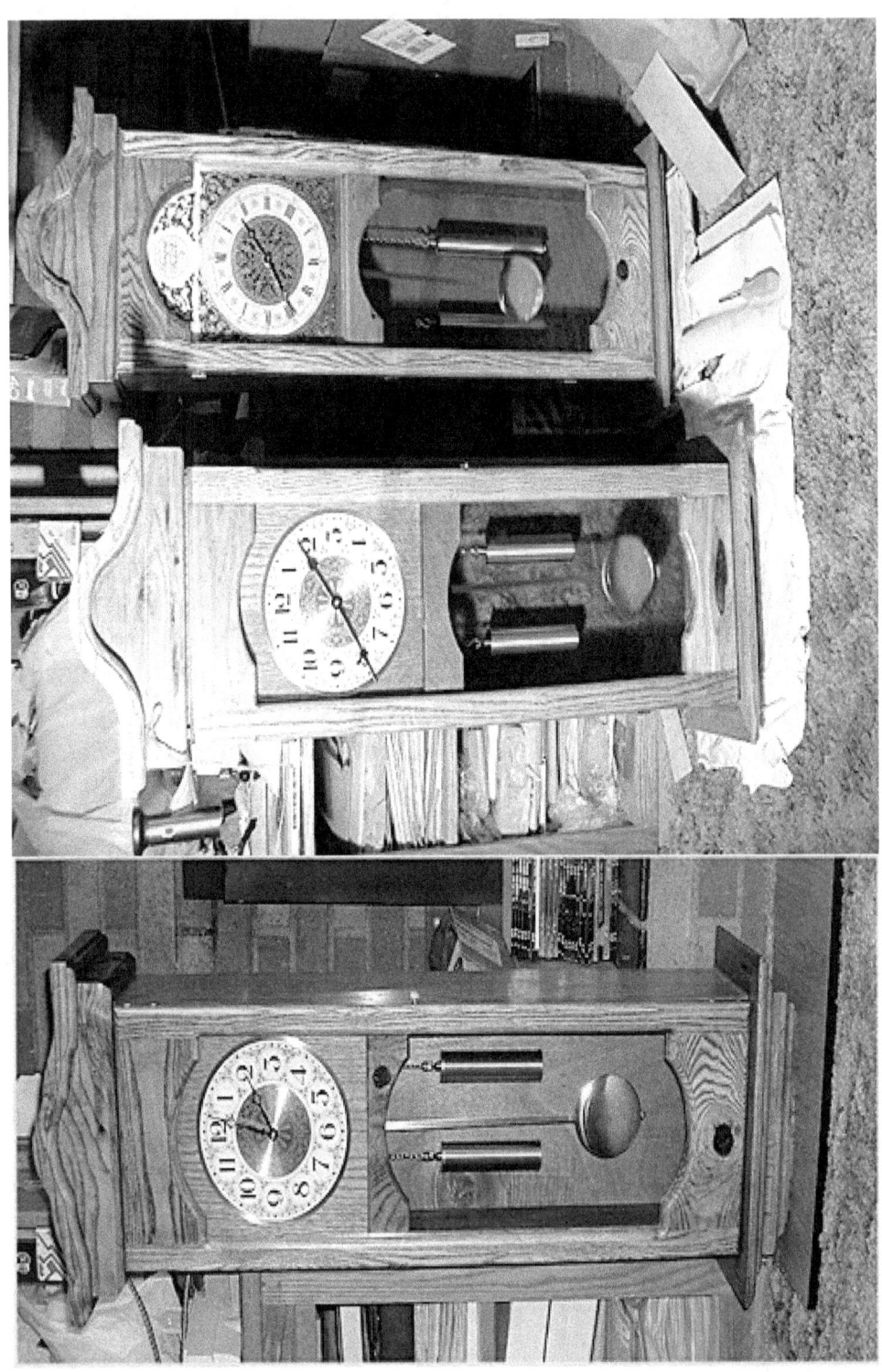

corners. Rout along one edge with the same decorative bit you will be using for the front molding. (Like a rounding over bit...) Cut two opposing 45 degree miter corners at the ends.

With your curve piece from above nicely smoothed, it is time for routing. Clamp securely. Just make careful small cuts, gradually working in until the bit guide is riding right against the curved workpiece.

At this point you should have the long side piece big enough for two side moldings, mitered and routed with the next step to match and miter the ends of the curved top molding.

Carefully center your front molding over the front of the inner sub molding on the clock. You should have excess at each end to allow for 45 degree miters at each side. Very carefully mark the inside of your curved molding at the corner of the clock box inner existing molding.
You want the ends to be perfect length for a perfect match to each side miter.

See Figure 15 for a general assembly of the upper molding over the previously glued inner sub molding. The critical elements here are to have nice miter joints, and a centered assembly plus one more item:

- **Allow an inside lip of about 5/16" by mounting the side and front molding above the edge of the inner sub molding.**

- This is so a fitted 1/4" Oak veneer may be applied neatly into the top recess..

Clamp and glue the moldings once you are happy with miters and parts placement. Wipe any excess glue from the surfaces, and allow the assembly to dry.

Once the assembly is dry, you can cut the 1/4" piece of Oak

veneer to fit into the upper surface on the clock.

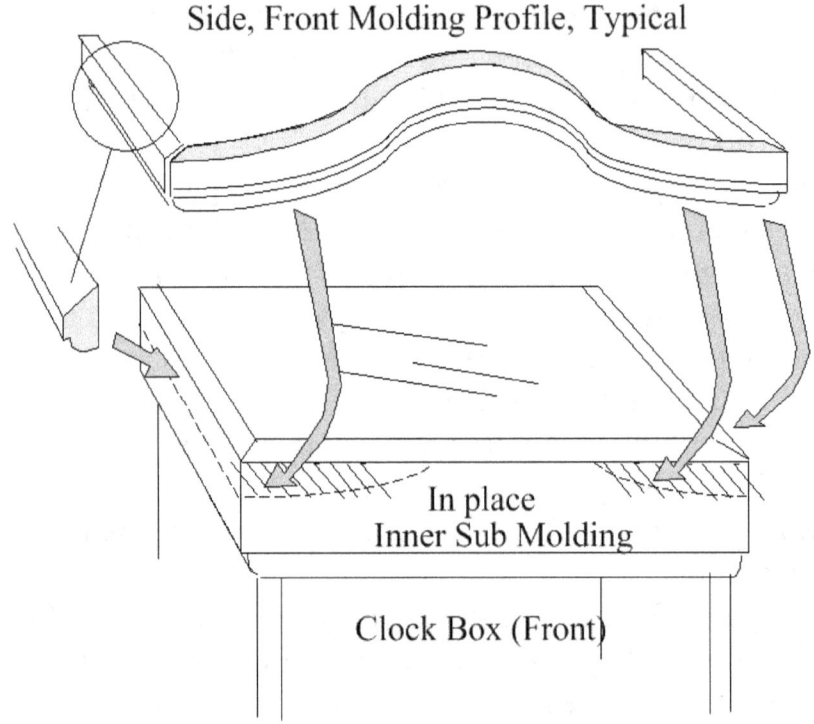

Fig. 15. Mounting top Molding

Cut and sand this piece to fit perfectly into the lipped area, then apply glue and put a weight on top to assist in gluing. Wipe off any excess with a damp paper towel... by now this should be automatic whenever you glue!

It is a good idea to dowel the curved moldings, just to insure strength because these or the inner moldings tend to be the lifting point when hoisting the clock onto the wall or while handling during the remainder of construction.

The miter corners of the inner sub molding (and at the rear on the inner sub molding into the clock box sides) were dowelled above.

Now do the same for the curved outer molding -actually the side pieces; anchor a dowel at the rear of each side into the sub molding, and add a corner miter dowel drilling from the side into the front curved molding. You can use a sharp chisel to carefully trim the dowels, but if you use an awl to gauge depth, there may be virtually no trimming. Be careful not to damage the surface of the moldings. These dowels lock the whole assembly to each other and to the box very substantially.

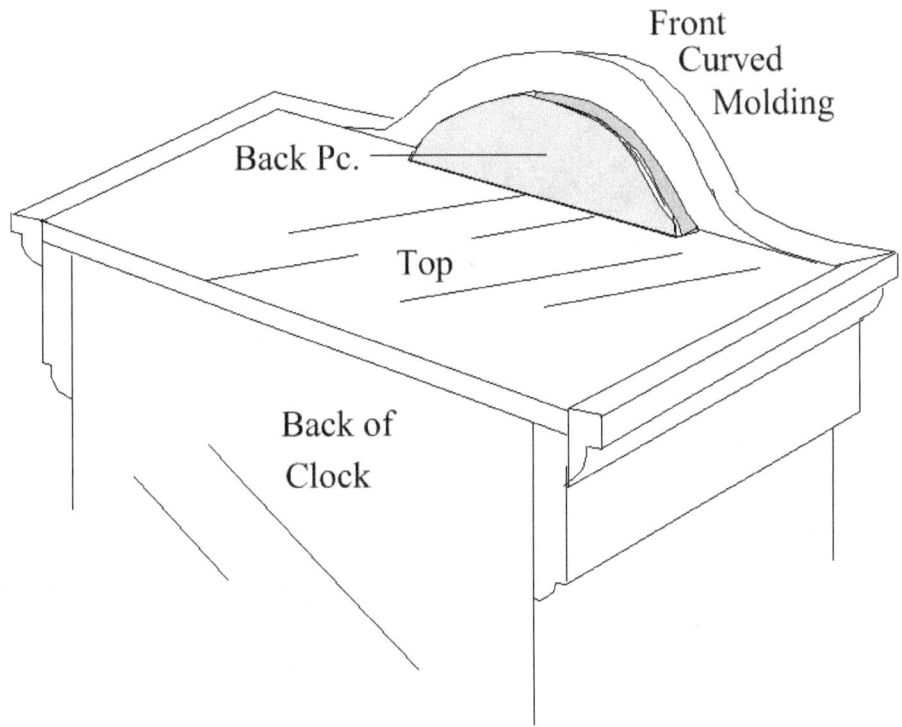

Fig. 16. Back Piece

There is a hole below the curved molding in front, use a piece of Ash or the Oak veneer cut into a curve to match to the outer molding curve, to cover this opening behind the outer curve. See Figure 16. Sand the upper curved edge to a nice appearance, and glue it on with nice grain showing on the front. Be very careful to clean off excess glue. If you use a thick piece of Ash, you may dowel it into the top as well for extra strength.

Use a wood filler in all finish nail holes as well as damaged areas, miter corner gaps, etc. Trim dowels to the surface where needed. Sand these areas smooth with very fine sandpaper.

Chapter 6

The Door Assembly

The door is basically a frame with a decorative top and bottom piece. There are two styles that look nice and are not too difficult to rout. Inside the frame is glass to allow the clock dial and pendulum and weights to show. The top and bottom crosspieces have an arc cut into the inside to match approximately to the dial curvature; this gives a complementary and pleasing effect . The outer front edge of the frame can be rounded clear round... or the sides can be routed like a column with an unrouted portion on the outer edge top and bottom matching to the inner opening.

One side of the door frame is dowelled or permanent; the other is removable to allow changing the glass should it ever get cracked.

Once pieces are cut to size and smoothed or sanded, the inside edge must be routed **prior to cutting the groove for the glass.** This is because the bit guide can indent into the weaker groove area and then damage the smooth curve around the inside edge of the frame.

Examine Figure 17 on the following page. You need a router circle guide for the upper and lower arcs, or actually you could cut them very carefully with a Jigsaw. If a Jigsaw is used the arc must be sanded smooth to provide a good guide for the router.

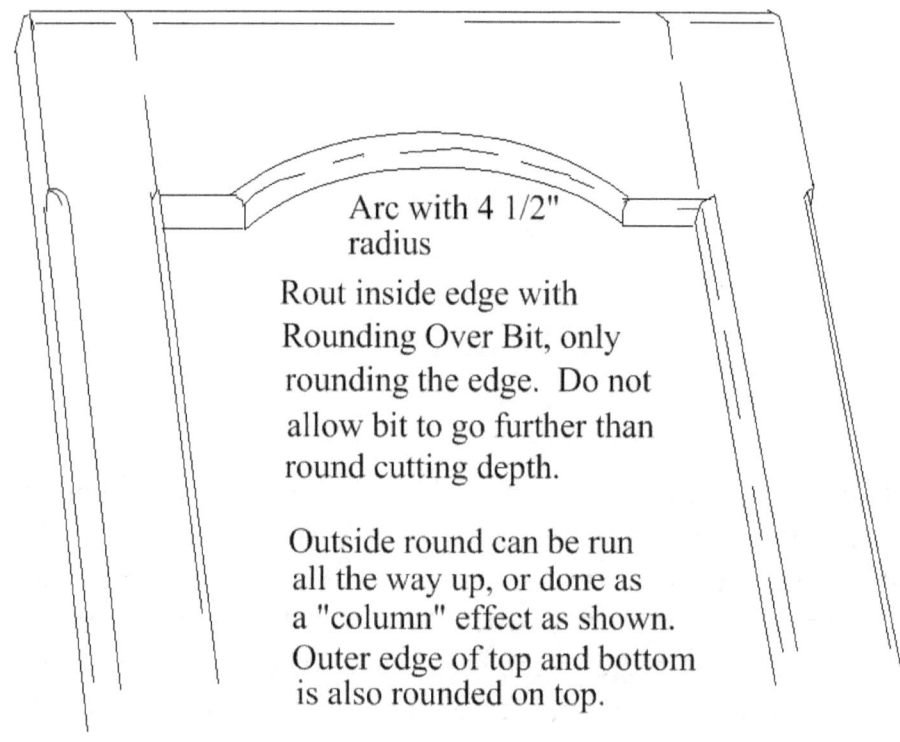

Fig. 17. Door Details

 To begin, rip two side frames of 3/4" thick Ash, about 1 5/8" wide, the length the same as the space between the top and bottom moldings on the clock body. Later you can trim the pieces to clearance for the door frame fit. Try to find a piece or two with a unique rot patch or knot, adding to the beauty and unique appearance that will set your clock off.
 Cut two door frame crosspieces of the same Ash, about 2 3/4" wide and about 8 1/4" long. You will rout or use a Jigsaw to cut a centered 4 1/2" radius arc into each piece; the arc should extend into the piece about 3/4" to 7/8" at the deepest arc point, the center. If you use the router, you will need the Edge/Circle

Guide attachment, but with care you can also do the job fine with a Jigsaw or Sabre Saw.

Router Method

If you use the Edge/Circle Guide attachment and router setup, there may be some shimming involved to match the height of the workpiece and router setup; be especially careful to clamp the workpiece securely. One way to do this nicely and also allow clamping out of the way of the router is to make two holding jigs of scrap wood approx 3/8" to 1/2" thick; some pieces of your 3/8" plywood are excellent. See Figure 18.

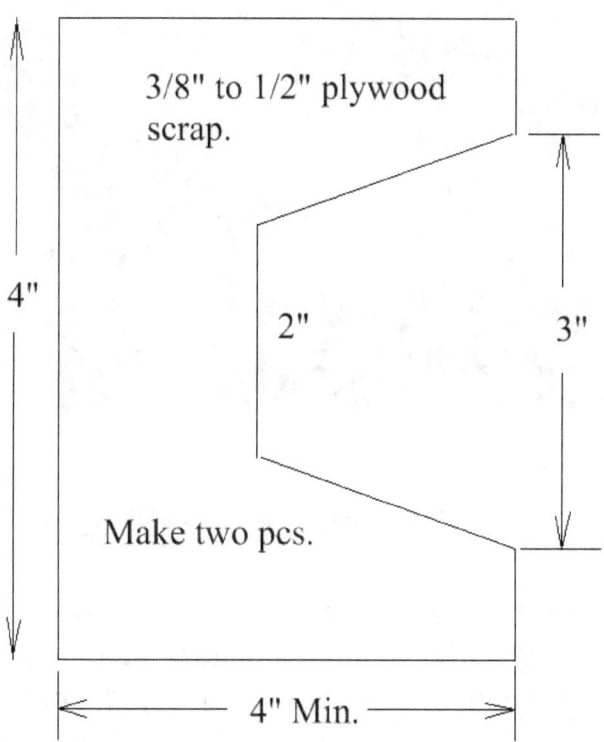

Fig. 18. Clamping Jig for Door Pieces

Fig. 19. Setup for Routing

The jig pieces are shoved inward and clamped to hold the door cross piece securely while routing. The weight of the router on top keeps the piece in place vertically during the process.

A scrap of 1/2" board with a pivot pin (nail) is used with the edge/ circle guide and router to produce the arc. Study Figure 19 to get the idea. The parts are clamped to the top of my table saw.

- Be sure to have the table saw **unplugged** during the router work.
- Remember, always... **unplug the router power cord before any bit installation!**

Use about a 1/4" straight cutting bit in the router. Tighten the collet and release the lock. Check the edge guide; the radius to bit center is ideal at about a 4 1/2" radius; set your guide accordingly.

Mount and clamp the pivot pin piece with the pivot nail upward and straight out at 90 degrees from the center of the workpiece. With the router and edge guide pivoted on the nail, be sure your arc cut will loop into the workpiece at the center about 3/4" to 7/8" deep.

You normally move the router in a clockwise manner about the pivot. That way the router bit is spinning opposite to the movement through the work. It won't grab and jerk into the wood, damaging your cut. So, on each pass you will begin at the left of your workpiece *just before the bit contacts the wood*. Make sure the router is securely supported throughout the arc movement and a bit beyond each side of the arc cut.

Plug the router in once ready. See Figure 20 on the next page for a general procedure view, then follow the listed steps carefully.

- Use small incremental depth adjustments of about 3/32" on each pass.

- Switch the router ON and keep a very slight outer tension as you push the router clockwise around the arc, *lighten a bit in the last inch of arc cut*. This is so you won't split off a portion of the edge. There is an ideal cutting speed movement through the wood; too slowly will burn the wood and bit, you will also sense a vibration if you push too hard.

Fig. 20. Making the Arc Cut

- Cut just past the right edge as the bit comes out of the wood.

- Then gently apply the slight outer tension and return the router counterclockwise back through your cut to the starting position.

- Drop the bit depth down about 3/32" and do successive passes in an identical manner.

As you reach within about 1/16" of cutting clear through the piece, stop your work, shut off the router, **unplug** and set aside. Use a sharp wood chisel to remove the waste and use a belt sander to carefully smooth the flashing to the edge of the arc.

  This process is only for the inner arc on the top and bottom door frame crosspieces. Only do the inner arc initially, the remaining outer and inner frame routing is done with the door assembled.

Sabre or Jigsaw Method

  First inscribe a 4 1/2" radius arc onto the center of the door piece, the depth of the max arc from the edge should be about 3/4" to 7/8" so as to leave about 1 1/2" approximate width at the center of the cross piece. Clamp the crosspiece securely and use a Sabre Saw with narrow blade at a lower speed to carefully cut the curve. At lower speed, the cut can be very precisely controlled. Then sand with a belt sander to smooth the cut, but be very careful not to damage the smooth curve.

Assembling and Finishing the Inner Edge of the Door Frame

Before routing the inner and outer door frame, you must assemble the door temporarily. After the routing process you will cut the glass slot in each piece, then dowel to make one side frame permanent with the crosspieces, leaving the other removable as a means for glass replacement if ever needed.

Sand the edges of your frame pieces to remove any blemishes or roughness. Then measure carefully to get an exact fit of the door width to the clock box. Trim the crosspiece parts as necessary to achieve the exact width of the door; leave the door height at about the space between the upper sub molding and the lower molding for door clearance. You can true it later once the door is assembled. Keep the arc centered in the crosspieces.

Fit and clamp the door frame in place on your bench with the ends matching so you can drill two holes into the corner of each side frame to attach the crosspieces. Check for squareness. **Keep in mind to drill to miss any future glass slot area!**

Drill initially with a 5/32" bit through the sides and deep into the crosspieces to allow for 2 1/2" deck screws. Redrill for screw clearance holes in the side frames only, then install the screws to hold all frame pieces correctly. Use 2 1/2" deck screws. Do not worry about the screw heads protruding at this point; you will be routing the *inner* portion of the frame.

- **Make sure the router is unplugged from power.** Remove the router edge/circle guide.

- Clamp the door frame to your work table.

- Install a 3/8" rounding over bit into the router. Tighten the collet to secure the bit.

- Set the bit depth as desired for producing a corner round. You can run only the quarter round to first see if you like the effect. Lay a short scrap board inside of the same thickness as the door as an inner support for the router base.

- Restore power to the router and rout the inside of the door frame. Rout left to right around the inner portion.

- If you decide you wish a bit of the ridge lip to show you can do so by slightly deepening the cut -you still have that option. But a simple corner round is just fine.

Cutting the Glass Slot

Next, it is time to slot for the glass inside the door. Take the door frame apart, marking each side of each corner in a manner to match them back once you cut for the glass. **Unplug power from the saw.**

- Set the table saw fence and blade depth to do a blade cut about 1/2" deep and about 1/4" from the back side of each frame piece. You will guide the back of each piece against the saw table fence to do the 1/4" spacing.

- Plug in power to the saw once you are ready.

- **Note: The side pieces are not slotted end to end.** When slotting the side pieces, slowly and carefully as you keep the back of each piece against the saw table fence, lower onto the blade so as to start the cut so it won't quite show at the end of the piece, then run it through the saw, stopping just before the blade would come out at the other end.

- The top and bottom crosspieces must be slotted all the way across. Simply guide these through the saw with the back side right against the saw table fence. Note you will have to raise the blade to get 1/2" clearance into the arc portion. **Be extremely careful here, make a jig or clamp a long block to the upper portion of the curved piece to ride upon the saw fence and support the curved side from dropping as it goes off the edge of the table.** Take some time to rig this safely! **Unplug the saw until you are ready.**

- After doing the pieces once, with a typical saw blade thickness, the glass slot will be almost 1/8" wide. You need slightly more than 1/8" for standard 1/8" glass, so move the table saw fence very slightly away from the blade to give perhaps 1/32" additional space. Test the first piece you cut with a piece of glass. Once you glue the parts of the frame together, those slots will be inaccessible for modification. So make sure the slot is sufficient. The frame has a way of becoming tighter once it is put together so a slightly loose glass fit is ideal.

Assembling and Routing the Outside of the Door

Reassemble the frame door using one screw at each of the matched corners. Check that the routed corners and upper surface are smooth at the joint. Take a careful measurement for the inside dimensions of the frame and add about 3/4 inch to the width and height values for a fit into the two 1/2" slots; that will insure a 1/4" gap clearance for the sheet of glass.

Get the glass sheet cut at a glass shop. Then with one side of the door removed, check that the glass goes in nicely and fits once the other side panel is reattached. If it does, the next step is dowelling the one side frame. Remove the glass.

With one screw holding each corner, you will have a free spot to drill for a 1/4" dowel on **each end of the one side frame**. Clamp securely so the pieces will not shift as you drill the holes. Drill each hole, and be very careful to avoid drilling into the glass slot of the top and bottom frame pieces. You can angle the holes, that is fine. Drill to get about 3/4" into the upper and lower frame pieces. Use an awl to measure into the hole and cut two dowels to fit. Unscrew the frame, apply glue to the joint, then into the dowel holes and a bit onto the dowel, push or tap the dowels in and replace your screws into the joints, tighten, check for squareness and flatness. Carefully wipe off excess glue with a damp paper towel. Let dry.

Once dry, remove the two screws and drill those holes for another dowel. Dowel the remaining holes, gluing and clamping, wipe off excess glue. You now should have the one side frame securely attached to the top and bottom frames.

When the assembly is solidly dry, use a wood chisel to remove any protruding dowels, and do a final edge sanding using a block of wood with the sandpaper to smooth.

Slide the glass in once more to check fit. If all looks good, you are ready for the other side frame mounting and to do outside routing of the door frame. Remove the glass.

You need to countersink the four screw holes in the other side frame. There are two ways you can do this, either with a countersink, or with a 3/8" blade bit run about 1/4" into the side frame holes. Mount the side frame with your screws (no glass inside...) and make sure the surface and joints are smooth on the front of the frame.

Fit the door to your clock, using the table saw Miter Guide set at 90 degrees (checked with a square...) measure the clock body and run a thin sliver off the top and bottom crosspieces on the table saw so the door fits between the upper and lower moldings with a small clearance top and bottom.

Now you are ready for routing the outer edge of the door frame. There are several considerations here:

- You can rout down each side frame all the way, or stop even with the inner corner to give a "column" look to the side frames. See picture opposite, Figure 21. This photo shows the column effect frame.

- If you do a nice job with the dowelling smooth and even on the edge, you can use the rounding over bit edge guide to route the one dowelled side frame; however **on the side frame with screws, you must clamp a guide board onto the door front to avoid the bit guide dropping into the screw countersink holes, which would damage the piece.** Use a 3/8" Rounding Over bit.

- It will help when doing the edges to have a scrap board the same thickness as the door to support the router at the outer edge of its base.

- Rout straight across the top and bottom crosspieces.

This should complete the clock body and door except for mounting the hinges.

The ornamental hinges are Stanley type 80-3460 . Mount the upper hinge at about 4" to 5" from the top of the door and the bottom hinge 5" to 6" respectively from the bottom of the door. Center the middle hinge halfway between these two. *Mark the location of each hinge on the rear of the door,* and draw an out-

Fig. 21. Clock Unfinished With Door

line of the decorative hinge at each. Use the router with a straight bit and a wood chisel to carefully remove the wood inside your outline to the depth of the hinge thickness. Check as you cut for a nice fit. Do this for all three hinges.

Set a hinge in place and mark with an awl to drill for the screws. When drilling into the door frame, first drill to screw depth with a 5/64" bit, about 1/2" deep; use a bit of masking tape on the bit to set the depth. Then replace with a 7/64" bit that is taped to drill to only a 1/8" depth. This should give a reasonable mounting for each hinge.

- As you set a screw to test the holes, do not twist with strength, but with extreme care, a broken screw is not a good thing here. **If a hole simply seems too tight, use a 3/32" bit for perhaps a tad past 1/8" depth to give some relief. Or gently wobble the 5/64" bit in the hole.**

- Do not try to twist the screws super tight, snugging so the hinge is secure is plenty.

- After testing the mounting of all three hinges you are almost ready to set the door on the clock body. One more step first.

- Look at Figure 22 opposite. On the back of the frame, side B, the hinge is mounted top side down with the factory countersunk side holes *down against* the frame back.. This is done so the A portion of the hinge can swing downward to mount onto the side of the clock box. So the holes in the hinge portion that will mount on the door should be countersunk a bit on the *other* side . At this point you are ready to reverse the hinges to the configuration described, and drill the holes to mount the door onto the clock body.

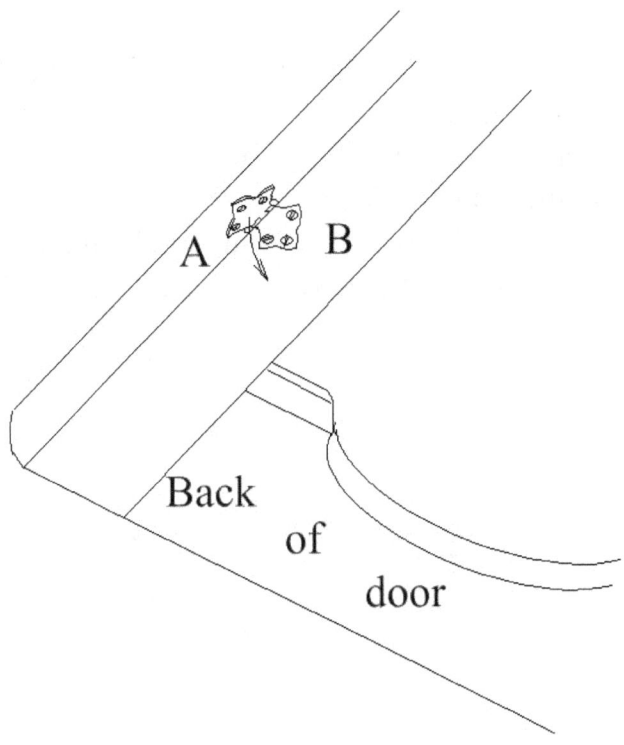

Fig. 22. Typical Hinge Mount

- Remove the hinges. On <u>one side</u> of the hinge, countersink the three holes *on the back side.* **Be careful not to apply the countersink too much so that the screw can fall through.**

- Remount the hinges, then set the door onto the clock box. Center it between the upper and lower molding, and very carefully mark the holes to drill to mount to the clock box. Drill as described above.

- Test mount the hinges.

- On the other side of the door a slight bit above the door frame center, judge where you wish to mount the Brass hook latch. This is Stanley part no. 803640 . You will need to glue a small block on the inside of the clock to mount the hook loop screws. The hook attaches to the door and loops into the hook loop mounted on the clock body.

Chapter 7

Finishing the Inside

Inside the clock is a framework which mounts the dial and is the support for the Brass Shell Weights. It is made up of light 3/4" x 3/4" wood strips, like Pine. It is a good idea to make an angular brace or thin plywood piece as part of both the horizontal and vertical sides of the frame, to provide strength and rigidity.

The front of the framework will be covered with a panel of 1/4" Oak veneer, which supports the dial. At the bottom of the panel will be a decorative arc crosspiece, similar to the cross frames in the door, to complement the lower area with the pendulum and weights.

First the basic framework must be fabricated. Basically make two rectangular framework assemblies as shown in Figure 23, *mirror images of each other.* Glue and clamp to form each rectangular frame. Add a triangular brace of the same 3/4" x 3/4" wood members on each one as shown. Make sure the individual units are square and match each other as you glue them. Spring Jaw Clamps are nice for this gismo.

You may also use screws at each joint too if you wish.

Next use a plywood scrap to attach the two mirrored parts together as shown.. Use a thin 1/4" to 3/8" plywood piece at one end about 3" wide, (this will eventually be at the top when the frame is mounted in the clock...) and cut the length so the framework is sized at about 1/4" less than the inside clock box width.

Set the unit on a flat surface and glue and clamp the plywood onto the one end, making sure of the spacing and checking with a square that the plywood and frame held true.

For the other end use a crosspiece of 1/2" plywood, about 2" in width... mount it about halfway down -- glue it onto the lower part of the frame. This piece will be the support for the Brass Weight Shells, hence the thicker plywood.

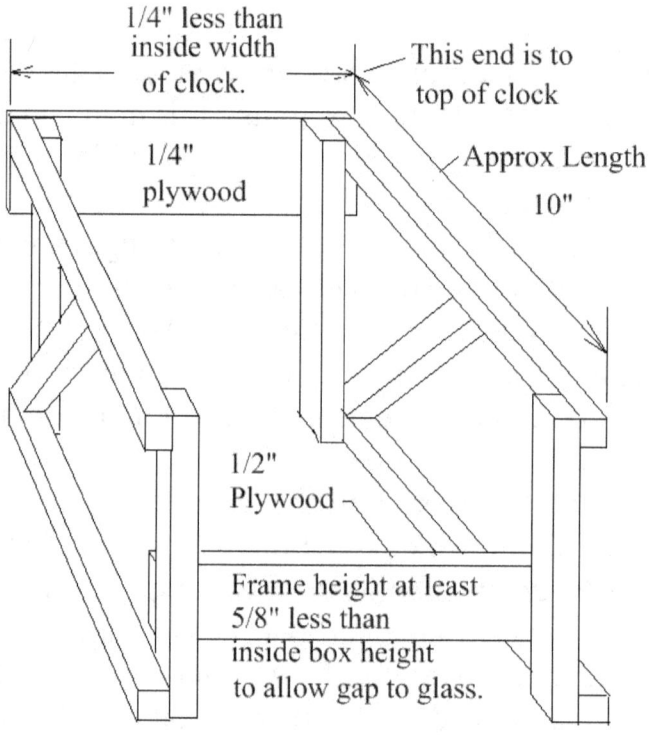

Fig. 23. Dial Support Frame

The Dial Panel

Measure the space between the clock sides on the inside. When you cut the 1/4" Oak veneer for the dial panel, cut its width about 1/8" less so it can easily go into the clock box. The grain should run vertically with the clock, not crosswise.

Before cutting the clock dial panel, you need to determine the length. Cut a large cardboard piece from a box to fit inside and lay over the framework inside. Set the framework inside the clock body and slide it to a position so the top crosspiece is about 1/2" below the upper inner sub molding. Slide the cardboard up to just below the clock box inner sub molding.

Without disturbing the frame or cardboard sitting in the clock box, close the frame door onto the clock body. Lay the dial centered on the cardboard and adjust it up or down so the dial sits below the door frame arc crosspiece an inch or two and pleasingly complements the arc crosspiece in the door. Adjust to your satisfaction.

Mark a location hole for the clock motor shaft. Next imagine a similar gap *below the dial* as that above. Put a mark on the cardboard, then put a mark about 1 1/2" below it. This length depicts the actual dial panel height and should be about the value you have marked from the top of the cardboard in inches; it can be trimmed later if needed. *If you look at some of the clock photos in this book, you will get the idea.*

Having the width and height now, you can cut the dial back panel from 1/4" Oak veneer. Drill the 7/16" hole for the clock motor shaft.

You will next cut a piece of 3/8" thick plywood veneer or 3/8" Ash, Oak, whatever-- in a width of about 2". It should be almost long enough for the width of the dial panel. This piece will have an arc cut to form the lower decorative arc crosspiece you see in the photos. It gives a balance to the upper panel and dial portion and also sets off a matching arc to the lower door frame

crosspiece and the pendulum and weights area in the lower part of the clock..
See Figure 24 for a detailed plan for the dial and lower piece.

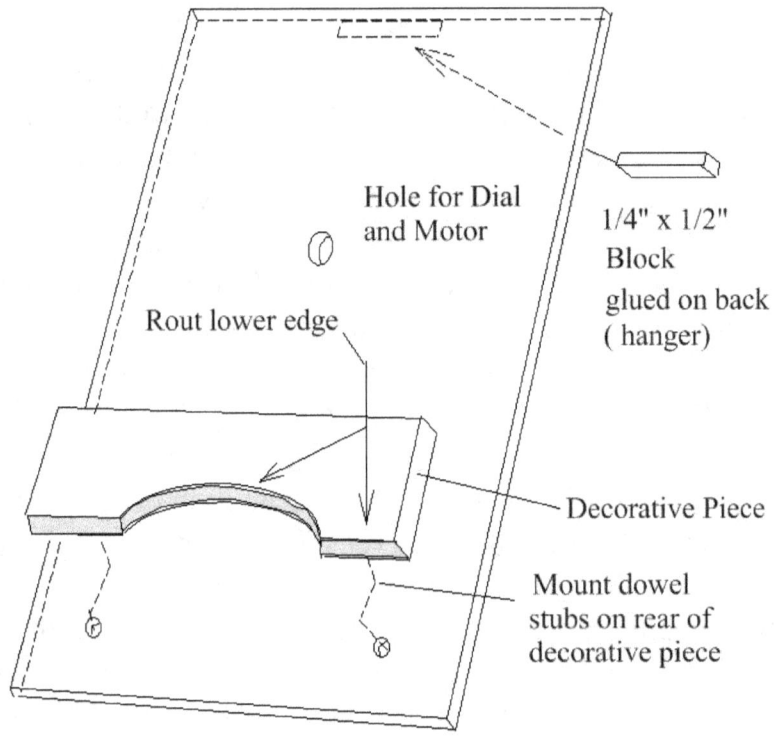

Fig. 24. Clock Dial Panel

Do the arc cut with a Jigsaw in the lower decorative piece, and sand carefully. Then rout across the top and bottom edge with a 1/4" corner round bit.

Drill two 1/4" holes in the back of the piece no more than 1/4" in depth and do matching through holes in the dial veneer. Add and glue short dowel stubs on the rear of the decorative piece, and you will be able to push the decorative piece into the holes in the dial panel for a friction fit.

Once you have the decorative piece made, you can trim the lower part of the panel off up to the top of the decorative arc.

It really dresses up the final appearance to cut a top arc piece, and two side pieces that fasten to the dial and essentially close in the dial area around the inner edge of the door frame. These pieces are glued onto the dial panel to set just beneath the edge of the door frame with a slight inset. See Figure 25.

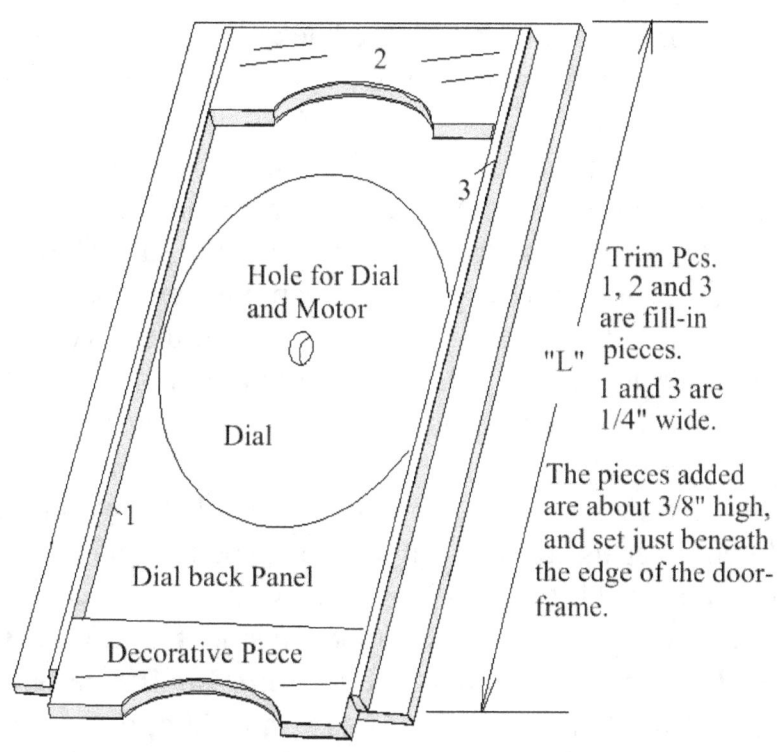

Fig. 25. Trim Details

Drill one hole on each side to connect the panel to the panel support frame with the upper hanger block touching the upper frame crosspiece. When the clock is upright on the wall, this hanger block will support the clock dial panel during removal for servicing the battery, etc.

Set the dial support framework into the clock box. Make sure the upper crosspiece is below the inner sub molding of the clock box. Check that the clock dial back panel will hang over the top of the frame crosspiece, yet the dial panel could be lifted forward and out once the frame is attached in the clock..

With the setup checked you can now drill through the clock back for attaching the frame. Take your time, make sure the frame is equidistant from each side; measure carefully and drill TWO holes for one side through the back of the clock box with a 5/32" bit, adequate clearance for #6 or #8 wood screws. Countersink these two holes.

Reset your dial support framework into the box, (with the upper crosspiece correct for hanging the dial) and center the lower side frame over the holes you drilled. When you are satisfied, slide the edge of the clock box over so you can push an awl up through the drilled holes in your clock box and mark your frame for drilling. Drill the two holes in the frame with a 3/32" or 7/64" bit-- if soft wood use the smaller size, if a harder wood use the larger.

Mount the frame into the clock with two 3/4" #6 wood screws, snug, do not over tighten. Use a piece of tape to mark a depth gauge on your drill bit of 3/4". Now very carefully measure for the two additional screws on the opposite side, **mark and drill through the rear of the clock box and into the frame back piece using the 3/32" or 7/64" bit as you hold against the front of the dial frame.** Mark your 5/32" bit with tape at a depth of 3/8", and drill just the clock box clearance holes. Countersink the holes. Run two 3/4" #6 wood screws into these holes to finish checking the frame mounting. Make sure the dial panel mounts correctly. If so, this completes the frame and dial panel.

Chapter 8

The Clock Finish

At least half the job in any woodworking is doing the finishing, the stain and varnish. I always had problem with this final step until I discovered the method described here.

You can do a beautiful job on building a project, but when you apply the stain it can suddenly go horribly wrong, dark and light irregular blobs on various grain patterns, glue spots showing where you failed to remove all carpenters' glue, a totally unprofessional finish that is embarrassing.

Sometimes on a wood piece, the grain is going parallel or along the surface of the wood, but sometimes it can be somewhat coming outward or going inward on the surface. Basically imagine the wood grain as a series of long wood fibers, they turn or lie flat depending on the blemishes, twists, and knots or burls in the wood. As boards are cut from wood they sometimes cross grains coming out of or going into the cut surface. These areas will absorb stain in a different fashion. If the grain is coming outward it will take stain in a very dark fashion, in short, like the *end grain* of a board, which always stains darker than the flat wood grain along the board.

However you can do a very easy process to minimize these exaggerated spots and help make the stain take more evenly over the entire clock. (or any project..) Grains will still show nicely, but the whole effect will look more even and professional. You will achieve this by first using a *Sealer*.

Before doing any finishing, you must first sand the finish carefully with a fine sandpaper to eliminate any blemishes. You can use a Palm Sander or sanding block for flat surfaces, you must do irregular parts by hand, some of the foam sponge sanding blocks now available are especially nice as they can form somewhat to any surface. Always sand *with* the grain and be careful not to damage or flatten the decorative curved routed surfaces. In using a sanding block, use sparingly and gradually rotate around a curved surface.
Dust the surfaces with a soft cloth.

Making and Applying the Sealer

In a clean metal container, mix paint thinner (Mineral Spirits) and Polyurethane varnish in approximately equal portions to make a sealer. The solution is a watery consistency, and can be applied easily to your entire project with a brush. Use it liberally on end grain areas, it will soak into the grain.

It is probably easiest with the clock to separate the various pieces and first paint the clock box inside and out, then do the other parts separately, the door frame, the clock dial panel and the inside panel frame assembly. Once the entire project has sealer applied, allow it to dry thoroughly.
I suggest overnight drying, more if the weather is cool or damp.

Once the entire clock and all assemblies are fully dry, you will want to do some hand "touch" sanding, very lightly and *using a well used piece of 400 to 600 grit wet and dry sandpaper. These grits are typically black, carbide sandpapers.*

The purpose in using a "used" piece is to avoid it being as strongly abrasive as a new sheet, so a good approach with a new sheet would be to do initial sanding on the back of the clock and inside, and the dial panel and framework... these are not critical areas and this will "use" the paper and dull the effect for later sanding of the outside and moldings of the clock..

On the outer portions of the clock, sand lightly but try not to miss any areas, use gentle sanding on all molding surfaces so as to avoid flattening. When completely done, wipe dust off the parts with a clean cloth. It is time for stain next.

Staining the Clock Parts

In my experience the lighter stains are more pleasing in general, I usually use Provincial in Minwax or some other major brand, but the choice is yours. Open the can of stain carefully and stir it thoroughly with a clean stirring stick; be sure to catch the very bottom of the can for settled pigment. I usually use a small cloth wadded into a ball and dip it onto the stain, then apply the stain to the workpiece.

Start with the dial panel. Apply stain to both sides and a wipe to the edges leaving the top wet and set aside. Do the same with the dial support frame but wipe it fairly dry. In staining, allow the stain to sit on the piece for about 10 to 15 minutes, and then wipe the surface, sometimes across the grain to fill grain pores, but the last pass should go *with* the grain... you will also learn to control this timing effect for a piece which stains lighter to some extent, to achieve a more even color. Or reapply a second coat of stain.

Do the door next. Then finally, the clock body; be careful not to miss areas, especially in the molding crevices. After a few minutes, wipe dry as you did for the dial panel. Let the stain dry overnight after wiping.

If any areas of the clock appear significantly lighter you can add one more application and gently wipe to blend in with other areas. Let dry overnight again.

Applying Grain, Artwork

Chances are you will note areas of the clock which still appear lighter, or additionally lack the grain patterns obvious in the Ash or Oak portions. Now comes a technique that is pretty unusual... you will apply India Ink as either a tinting wash *with the grain* or actual wood grain lines!

At a craft store, obtain a small bottle of India Ink, as used for ink artwork. Also get a small tip art type paint brush and a Crow Quill point ink pen tip and holder. You will use some ink straight from the bottle and some watered down, as a tint.

Back at your workplace, in a small capped container like a pill bottle, mix a bit of half ink and half water. Do not fill the bottle; leave space for even more water. This will be a tinting solution and you may even water it down more, depending on your preference.

Any place you applied wood filler you will note the stain doesn't highlight the wood grain, as in blemished spots or finish nail holes. And on the decorative bottom molding, which is usually found mostly in Hemlock, there will be *no significant wood grain at all.* So you will use your ink wash and pure ink to simulate some portions of a simulated wood grain on these pieces.

On nail fill areas usually you need a hint of grain, nothing more. (No tint...)

In certain areas here and there on the Hemlock molding, put a 2 to 4" smear of your ink wash lengthwise on the piece... water as necessary to get a slightly darkened, yet transparent appearance to the occasional smears. Don't overdo it, just put in a few smears. Allow to dry.

Next, after it dries, use the Crow quill pen with the pure full strength India ink, and copy a few intermittent lines or specks of grain pattern lengthwise here and there on the Hemlock or any spots on the clock pieces where you wish to supplement the bare areas. Try to copy something similar to the Ash or Oak grain patterns that are on the other parts of the clock. Do not overdo, a few suggestion patterns similar to the actual Ash grain along with some darker tint patterns will do nicely, less is better than more in this case. The human eye somehow sees some of the patterns and sort of fills in the rest. If you get the hang of this, at some point you will be amazed at how the Hemlock or other areas blend right in with just some hints of grain pattern. That is a good stopping point. Once satisfied, let the whole setup dry thoroughly, preferably overnight. When the Polyurethane spray is applied, it will look even better. An excellent illusion!

Polyurethane Spray Varnish

Get a couple spray cans of Polyurethane Varnish, you have three choices here to suit your preference:

- Gloss
- Semi-Gloss
- Matte Finish (simulates a hand rubbed finish..)

In spraying the clock parts, be cautious to spray outside in a fresh air location. Do not spray anywhere near cars or anything that could be damaged by overspray, also spray only on a warm, dry day. Use a dust mask and glasses and avoid breathing spray. Place the item to be sprayed flat upon an empty cardboard box or bucket.

Spraying the small dial panel, the door frame and the panel framework will go quickly. Follow directions on the can: light coats, even movement as you spray, etc. Spray only one flat surface at a time. Several thin coats are better than a heavy one!

On edges you can do a few fast, light coats with time between. Let dry, then do the clock box body, one flat surface, perhaps the top or bottom very thin horizontally from a bit further away, a very quick light spot spray, **you do not want to cause runs!** Be very cautious near vertical edges.

The idea here is to spray the entire outer surface of the clock and door frame with about three to five spray coats, letting each coat dry thoroughly. (But two is fine for the dial panel and inside frame and surfaces.) Once the final precoat is dried thoroughly you are ready to do the last coat.

Final Finish

You should now have several coats on the clock. The next and final finishing step involves a gentle **wet hand sanding** with the "very used" 400 to 600 grit sandpaper. Using the 50-50 Paint Thinner and Polyurethane Varnish, (our homemade sealer) with a final very light sanding will remove any minor dust specks, fuzz or bugs that managed to stick into the varnish coats preceding.

Do the inside first and then wipe it with a ball of clean cloth wet with the sealer. Wipe with the grain. Let it dry and mount the dial panel support framework inside. The inside is finished except for the dial panel.

Always use a wood sanding block wrapped with the used sandpaper for the flat surfaces, and sand lightly, not to remove the varnish.... and use a gentle touch with sandpaper on the fingers for the molding rounds. Keep wet with the sealer during the sanding then wipe off with a clean rag slightly moistened in the sealer right after sanding. Wipe *with the grain.*

Now, this is the rule:
As you do an outer portion, immediately set it out and spray on a final Polyurethane coat. Remember to stay clear of any surface that could be damaged, spray outdoors clear of everything.

Do the top and one side of the clock and wipe off the surface, then immediately spray it with the final coat. Let it dry thoroughly.

Next do the bottom molding and other side; immediately spray it too. There will be some manipulation required to catch all surfaces but this last spray should put a very fine finish all round. Be sure to dry thoroughly before any shifting.

This avoids any further dust and leaves a very fine final finish. Do the dial panel and set aside.

After a day or so drying time check the finish over, it should be quite smooth and a very even professional looking job. Wipe with a soft cloth to remove an occasional dust hair sticking up, seems like there will always be a few, but having been sprayed with varnish, they will simply break at the surface and wipe off. The finish should be very nice.

Check Figure 26 through 28 following. They show several different clocks, illustrating some top molding patterns I have used. Even though Figure 27 has a clock similar to Figure 28, note the distinctive knots and unique rot patterns; these are two different clocks.

Always try to pick your wood pieces with distinctive beautiful knot and swamp rot patches, they show the beauty and uniqueness of fine woods. If woods did not have such features, you might as well use particleboard and fake grain... wouldn't that be a sad and pathetic choice!

Fig. 27. Two Styles

Fig. 28.

Chapter 9

Final Assembly

We are ready to assemble the clock. If not already in place, mount the inner framework assembly.

Each dial comes with a peel-off protective plastic sheet; remove it and set the dial in place on the Oak dial panel. Place a rubber washer onto the shaft of the Westminster Motor if supplied. Then push the shaft upward from the back, through the dial panel and dial; add the small brass washer and nut and snug finger tight as you true up the dial top to bottom, so the numbers are in the correct position.

Gently tighten a quarter to 1/2 turn more perhaps; be cautious, you do not want to strip the brass ferrule from the motor!

At the bottom of the inner dial framework, you need to mount two small screw in picture hooks, these will support the two Brass Weight Shells. There is a bit of guessing here on location.. the weights must hang behind the Pendulum on the clock motor.

On my clocks I found the distance from the hooks *to the back* should be set about halfway back from the pendulum position.

From each clock box side, I used a spacing of approximately 3". Mark and use an Awl to make a slight hole into the bottom framework crosspiece at each side in your designated positions. Mount the screw hooks temporarily, and screw them in slightly. Attach the pendulum to your dial and motor assembly, and temporarily attach it into the clock. Hook the chains onto your weights and adjusting the lengths, attach to the hooks. Check the appearance with the clock held upright, and adjust the frame hook positions if desired. Once satisfied, screw the hooks into the frame crosspiece until they are nice and solid.

Each weight should hang down about half way in the open area behind the pendulum; you will find a pleasing appearance in there somewhere and can remove most of the excess brass finish chain. You can pinch the brass hooks closed so the chain is secure if you wish.

Take the door frame apart and install the glass. Mount the door using the brass hinges you pre-drilled for earlier. Be careful tightening the brass screws .. you must not break one off in the hole. Enlarge the holes slightly if needed. Carefully mount the hook latch to complete the door assembly onto the clock.

Mount the dial panel after installing the battery into the motor. Wipe the clock off nicely and it is ready to wall mount. Use a 3" deck screw into a stud, for wall mounting. The clock is under 20 lbs and the screw supplies plenty of support.

Chapter 10

Mantel Style Clock

To make a mantel clock rather than a wall clock, you must downsize the entire clock. The same attractive dials are available in smaller sizes, like 4 1/2" and 6" or so; www.Norkro.com has several sizes.

I would suggest the 4 1/2" size. This would proportion to a clock width of about 7" using a frame door with 1 1/4" maximum frame widths. With scaling of the rest of the clock, a height of about 20 to 22" seems reasonable.

The curved top and associated sub inner molding would be done similar to the wall clock except in smaller scale to match the clock.

The main change beyond scaling is the base of the clock; instead of the very bottom smaller than the main clock, the reverse is true; the bottom base is expanded to give stability. Similar moldings to those used for the wall clock are certainly a usable approach, and simply setting the moldings outward at the bottom will give the needed stability.

I have not made any mantel type clocks at this time but will probably do one sooner or later as people have expressed interest in that style. Take a look at Figure 29 on the next page.

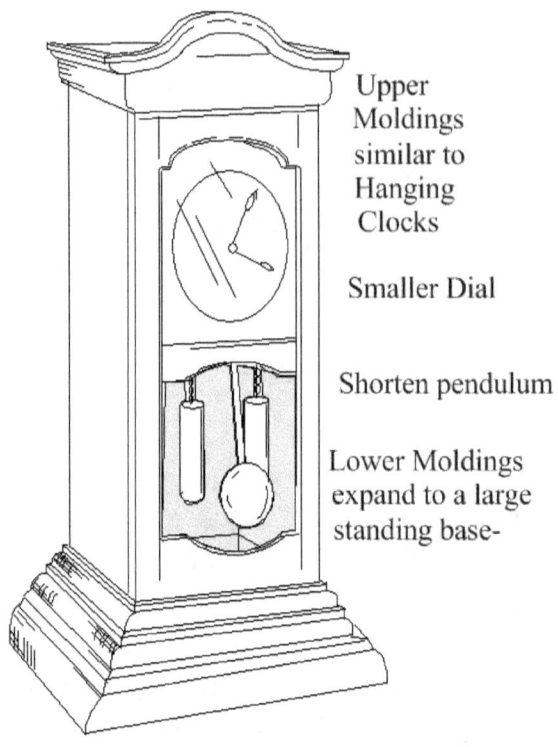

Fig. 29. Mantel Style Clock

That gives you an idea for Mantel type clocks, so you now have a good background and a general path towards your own clock building!
Be safe in your work, always take time to plan ahead.
Have fun and good luck!!

www.ingramcontent.com/pod-product-compliance
Lightning Source LLC
Chambersburg PA
CBHW051214290426
44109CB00021B/2452